CW01510479

Do All Knights Have Gallant Steeds?

Learning about Knights and their Horses

Ancient History Books

Children's Ancient History

BABY PROFESSOR

EDUCATION KIDS

Speedy Publishing LLC

40 E. Main St. #1156

Newark, DE 19711

www.speedypublishing.com

Copyright 2017

All Rights reserved. No part of this book may be reproduced or used in any way or form or by any means whether electronic or mechanical, this means that you cannot record or photocopy any material ideas or tips that are provided in this book

Do All Knights Have Gallant Steeds?

Learning about Knights and their Horses

Ancient History Books

Children's Ancient History

BABY PROFESSOR

EDUCATION KIDS

Speedy Publishing LLC

40 E. Main St. #1156

Newark, DE 19711

www.speedypublishing.com

Copyright 2017

All Rights reserved. No part of this book may be reproduced or used in any way or form or by any means whether electronic or mechanical, this means that you cannot record or photocopy any material ideas or tips that are provided in this book

In the Middle Ages in Europe, especially from about 900 to 1500 CE, the most powerful fighting unit was the knight. We imagine him riding his gallant horse, charging the enemy or competing in a tournament. Read on and learn about knights and their horses of medieval Europe.

A Hero on a Horse

The knight in the Middle Ages in Europe, was the king's best weapon. Foot soldiers were not all that well trained, and once the enemy got close to archers, the archers could not protect or defend themselves well.

Artillery in those times was basically different devices that could throw rocks. They were slow and inaccurate, although given time they could beat down the wall of an enemy's castle.

But the knight trained for war with many weapons and was equipped to be unstoppable on attack and really tough on defence. The knight on the field of battle had powerful weapons and strong armor, but that meant he was carrying a lot of weight. People without armor could just run away from a knight if he was walking toward them.

A knight standing on the ground is pretty effective because he has trained hard and is a master of many weapons. But his full value as he serves his king and country only comes into play when he is armed and armored, and seated on his horse.

Knights' Horses

We think of knights on some sort of super-horse, maybe like the Clydesdales and Percherons that we may have seen at circuses or pulling beer wagons. But those huge breeds did not exist in the Middle Ages.

Breeders developed breeds of horses to carry and support the knight in battle several times over the medieval period, and those breeds died out when they were no longer needed.

Big horses cost a lot to feed, and if you don't have knights riding around on them any more (because foot soldiers have guns that can pierce knights' armor), then breeders don't keep raising and feeding big horses.

The rule of thumb is that a horse can carry about 30% of its own weight. So a small horse weighing about 850 pounds could carry a rider wearing 35 pounds of chain mail and carrying a lance and sword.

This is the sort of horse and rider we see in the Bayeux Tapestry, which shows the invasion of England and the Battle of Hastings in 1066. We would see a horse like this in a farmer's field today (without the knight!) and it would look like an everyday horse.

As the weight of weapons and armor increased, breeders needed to develop stronger horses, and that usually meant bigger horses. By the 13th century, manuscripts start to talk about the "Great Horse", or "Destrier", which knights would ride into battle. "Destrier" probably comes from the Latin word for "right" or "right-handed", but we aren't sure why people used that name for this type of horse.

A normal riding horse in the thirteenth century was a "palfrey". A Destrier would be taller (about 68 inches, or 17 "hands" at the shoulder) and shaped like a Percheron of today. It weighed between 1200 and 1500 pounds, which means it could carry 400 pounds or more. That would be more than a knight in full plate armor, with lance, sword, and shield, would weigh.

By the 16th century smaller, more agile horses were needed for the battlefield, and such Great Horses that still remained only appeared in ceremonial events, like jousts in tournaments.

The best horse for a knight, no matter what its breed, had a round, dense body with a broad back. It had long legs with solid bones, and powerful muscles. The color of the horse rarely mattered, but the horse's spirit and temperament were very important. For the knight, the horse was more than transportation: it was an ally and a companion in life-and-death situations.

A knight would have not one, but a whole "string" of horses. Some would be palfreys for everyday riding, some would be fast horses for scouting and carrying messages, and the knight would have more than one war horse if he was going into battle. Horses could be injured or killed under the knight, and horses got tired. If there was a second battle the next day, the knight had to rest the horse he had used in the first battle, if possible.

You can see that having so many horses would be very expensive. Being a knight required having resources to pay for the armor for yourself and your horse, food for the both of you, and stablehands and squires to keep the horses healthy and ready for whatever task would lie before you.

Training a Knight's Horse

When a horse was about four years old, he was old enough to train for war. In Europe, knights almost always rode into battle on male horses. In the Middle East, the cavalry preferred mares.

Training for war and battle is very different from training for riding across a peaceful field, but there are some basics that are the same. The horse must be willing to do what the rider wants it to do, without hesitation. It needs to be able to go near other horses without getting distracted or getting into fights.

Required Skills for a Knight's Horse

Change of Gait and Direction

How quickly can the horse go from a walk to a trot, and from a trot to a gallop? How quickly can it stop? How quickly and well does it respond when the rider suddenly wants it to go right, then left? The horse has to learn to take directions just from the pressure of the rider's knees, since the knight might have his hands full of weapons and shields, and would not be able to tug on the reins. Stirrups, to encourage the horse to go faster, arrived along with the full heavy armor of the 14th century.

Working with an Armed Rider

The horse has to learn to carry a rider who is holding a long lance and trying to hit something with the point of it, or swinging a sword. Horses can be startled by sudden movements above them and near their eyes (as you and I might be!), and a horse that flinches and shies away can quickly throw its rider.

Change of Gait and Direction

How quickly can the horse go from a walk to a trot, and from a trot to a gallop? How quickly can it stop? How quickly and well does it respond when the rider suddenly wants it to go right, then left? The horse has to learn to take directions just from the pressure of the rider's knees, since the knight might have his hands full of weapons and shields, and would not be able to tug on the reins. Stirrups, to encourage the horse to go faster, arrived along with the full heavy armor of the 14th century.

Working with an Armed Rider

The horse has to learn to carry a rider who is holding a long lance and trying to hit something with the point of it, or swinging a sword. Horses can be startled by sudden movements above them and near their eyes (as you and I might be!), and a horse that flinches and shies away can quickly throw its rider.

Troop

The horse needs to learn to line up with other horses and basically ignore them, concentrating only on its rider. It has to be able to travel with many other horses without getting into fights or crushing some rider's leg between it and the next horse.

At the next level, the horse has to learn to move in formation with other horses—advancing, wheeling right and left, and, above all, charging across a field.

Distractions

The horse has to know to ignore sharp, sudden noises ranging from shouts to bangs to trumpets, the sudden appearance and disappearance of people and other horses and odd, unpleasant smells. Knights would spend many hours in mock-battles with other mounted knights so the horses would not be startled or even try to run away when it really mattered.

Facing the Enemy

A horse has to learn how to ride toward men who are holding long poles and other strange objects in their hands, without shying away; and to crash right into those men if that's what the rider wants. One of the hardest things at first for a horse is to not be nervous of a pike or a lance with a banner flapping and snapping at its tip.

The knight spends many hours training the horse first with people standing still in the training ring, then with those people holding poles, then with flapping flags at the end of those poles. The goal is to give the horse confidence that it is meeting something it has met before, so it can concentrate on doing what the rider wants.

Beyond that, the horse had to learn how to tell friend for enemy, and to bite and kick at the enemies. It might learn to rear up and crash its front hooves down on soldiers beneath it who might be trying to cut or entangle the horse's legs.

Armor for the Horse

Just as the knight wore strong and heavy armor into battle, so did the horse. The armor for horses was called "barding." It was made of panels of steel held together with heavy leather.

The full armor would cover the horse's neck, head, body, and chest. Sometimes the headpiece for the horse would have a horn sticking out, as if the horse were a unicorn! A decorated, padded cloth, or "trapper", covered the armor and the horse's hindquarters.

History is Interesting!

There's a lot more to learn about the way people lived and what they did in the past. For the Middle Ages, read the Baby Professor books Why Were Castles Built? and The Daily Struggles of People in the Middle Ages to explore further.

Visit

BABY PROFESSOR
EDUCATION KIDS

www.BabyProfessorBooks.com

to download Free Baby Professor eBooks
and view our catalog of new and exciting
Children's Books

Milton Keynes UK
Ingram Content Group UK Ltd.
UKHW051126030924
447802UK00003B/83